Look-Alike Animals

IS IT AN ALLIGATOR OR A CROCODILE?

by Susan B. Katz

PEBBLE
a capstone imprint

Pebble Sprout is published by Pebble, an imprint of Capstone.
1710 Roe Crest Drive
North Mankato, Minnesota 56003
www.capstonepub.com

Library of Congress Cataloging-in-Publication Data
Names: Katz, Susan B., 1971- author.
Title: Is it an alligator or a crocodile? / by Susan B. Katz.
Description: North Mankato, Minnesota : Pebble, [2022] | Series: Look-alike animals | Audience: Ages 5–8 | Audience: Grades K–1 | Summary: "Two beady eyes peek out of the water. Is it a crocodile or an alligator? They may look similar, but these two reptiles have many differences, including where they live and the shape of their snout. Let's find out what fearsome creature is really lurking below the water and explore their differences. The engaging text and stunning photos are perfect for early learners"—Provided by publisher. Identifiers: LCCN 2021002421 | ISBN 9781663908513 (hardcover) | ISBN 9781663908483 (pdf) | ISBN 9781663908506 (kindle edition) Subjects: LCSH: Alligators—Juvenile literature. | Crocodiles—Juvenile literature. Classification: LCC QL666.C925 K387 2022 | DDC 597.98/4—dc23 LC record available at https://lccn.loc.gov/2021002421

Image Credits
Alamy: Gary Brewer, 21; Newscom: Danita Delimont Photography/ Greg Johnston, 19; Shutterstock: Adam Morse 2, 31, Andrea Izzotti, 26, Anna_Kova (design element), cover (middle) and throughout, Arthur2002, 6, Catchlight Lens, 29, Chonlapoom Banharn, 10–11 (top), Cindy Larson, 18, Danny Ye, 30, DimaSid, 4, Gaston Piccinetti, cover (bottom), J.A. Dunbar, 7, James John Newton, 3, Junker Photography, 28, Kletr, cover (top), Marius Dobilas, 12, mark higgins, 15, Mark_Kostich, 20, Martin Mecnarowski, 14, Michael Zech Fotografie, 10–11 (bottom), Moehring, 22, Natalia Saudi, 5, Paco Como, 25, Piotr Velixar, 9, Rossar Williams, 13, Rudy Umans, 23, Simon Dux Media, 16–17 (bottom), Svetlana Foote, 24, Tibor Biro, 27, wildestanimal, 16-17, (top), William Silver, 8

Editorial Credits
Editor: Christianne Jones; Designer: Elyse White; Media Researcher: Svetlana Zhurkin; Production Specialist: Laura Manthe

KENNEDY

Swish!

Splash!

A large reptile thrashes its tail back and forth. It has scaly skin and a long body. Can you guess if it is an **alligator** or a **crocodile?** These reptiles look **similar,** but they have many **differences.**

Let's investigate!

See the shape of their snouts?

alligator

crocodile

Look closely. Alligators and crocodiles both have letter-shaped snouts. The rounded, **U-shaped** snout belongs to the gator. The pointy, **V-shaped** snout belongs to the croc.

What color is a croc?

crocodile

ISBN: 9781663908513

Title: Is it a Alligator or Crocodile?

Author: Katz, Susan B.

Price: 21.99

Date: 09/07/21

Kennedy

Penworthy

Can you see the shade of the gator?

Crocodiles are lighter in color than alligators and look more **olive** or tan. Alligators are mostly **dark black** or **gray.** There are no green gators like you see in cartoons.

alligator

Chomp!

Chomp!

Both animals have

sharp, knife-like teeth.

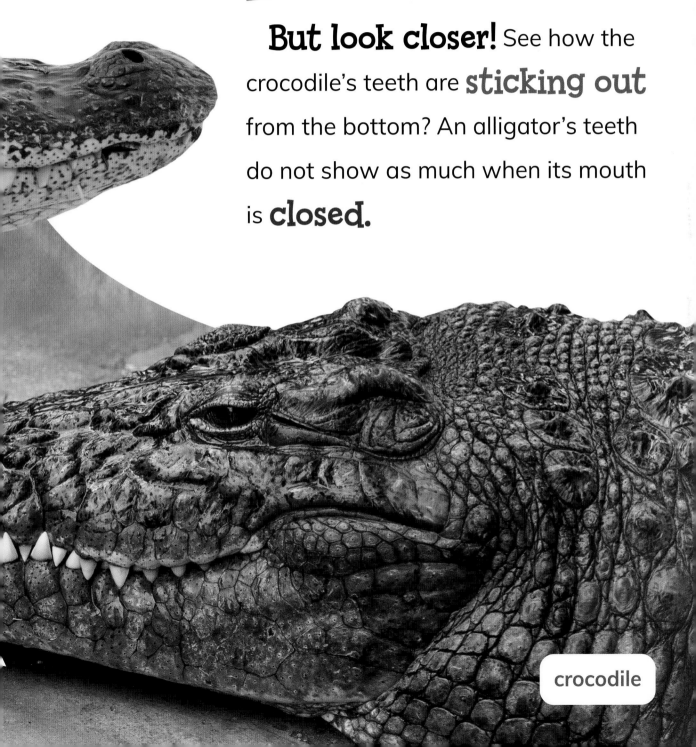

But look closer! See how the crocodile's teeth are **sticking out** from the bottom? An alligator's teeth do not show as much when its mouth is **closed.**

crocodile

Let's

size

them up!

crocodile

alligator

The largest gator was around **1,000 pounds (454 kilograms)** and **20 feet (6 meters)** long. It could stretch across a tennis court net!

Crocodiles grow to be several feet longer and weigh up to 1,000 pounds more than alligators. The biggest croc ever was as heavy as a hippo. It was around **2,000 pounds (900 kg)** and longer than two cars bumper to bumper at **23 feet (7 m)!**

Steer clear!

crocodile

With all those **sharp teeth,** both alligators and crocodiles are **very dangerous.**

But a croc is more likely to attack than a gator. Not only are crocodiles bigger, but their bites are **stronger** and **deadlier.** Alligators are **less aggressive** and usually **run away** from humans.

alligator

On your mark,

get set, go!

crocodile

Both animals move quickly on land and in water, but an alligator is **faster.** It can **sprint** up to

30 miles (48 kilometers) per hour!

Crocodiles can **gallop** and can **lunge** forward very far. Gators can **jump** up to

6 feet (1.8 m) in the air!

alligator

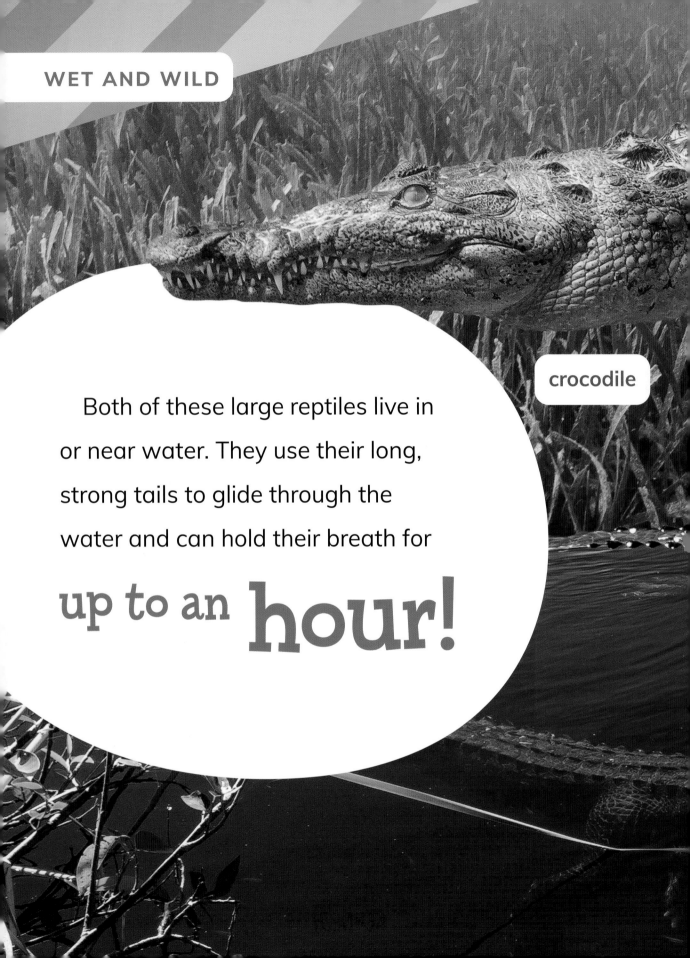

crocodile

Both of these large reptiles live in or near water. They use their long, strong tails to glide through the water and can hold their breath for **up to an hour!**

Crocodiles live in **saltwater seas** and **oceans** or **freshwater.**

Alligators only live in **freshwater** like **marshes** and **rivers.**

alligators

Florida is known for sun, fun, and some really **big** reptiles!

alligator

Alligators and crocodiles only soak in the sun **together** on the tip of **south Florida.**

Alligators live in **10 U.S. states** and **China.** So you are more likely to see an alligator than a crocodile in the United States. Crocodiles are found **around** the **world.**

crocodile

Make no bones about it—

alligator and crocodile legs are different lengths.

alligator

Alligators have **shorter** bones in their legs than crocodiles. That is why crocodiles can **gallop** and alligators cannot.

crocodile

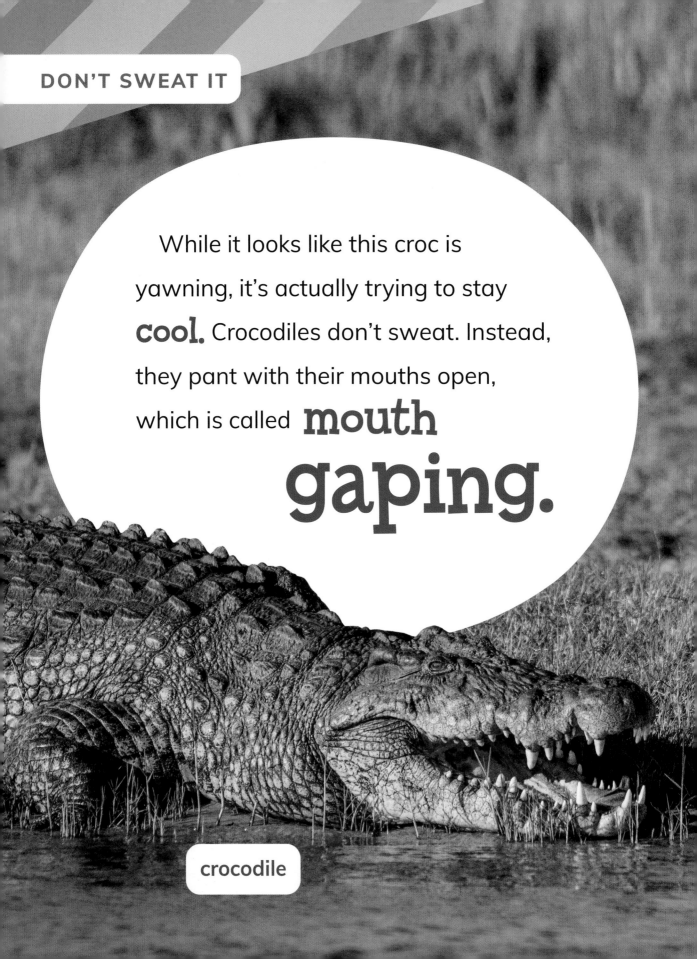

While it looks like this croc is yawning, it's actually trying to stay **cool.** Crocodiles don't sweat. Instead, they pant with their mouths open, which is called **mouth gaping.**

crocodile

Alligators would rather **cool off** in the **water** or the **shade.** Then they lay in the sun to warm up again.

alligator

What's on the daily **marsh menu?**

Lots of **meat!**

Alligators and crocodiles eat meat like **fish, snakes, turtles,** and **birds.**

alligator

crocodile

Neither animal can chew. They **grab** their prey, or **bite off** chunks, and **swallow** it whole. Crocs **thrash** their body around to help break food into smaller pieces.

alligator

Keep an eye out!

Both crocs and gators have eyes on the top of their heads to **search** for prey and **watch** for predators.

They are on the **lookout** for hungry jaguars, leopards, and slithering snakes. Both have **sharp night vision** for hunting prey after dark.

crocodile

Mama gators and crocs **lay eggs** and **bury** their nests near water. A mama stays near her eggs for up to three months, **protecting** them from predators.

alligator

When she hears her babies **chirp** from inside their eggs, she waits for them to hatch. Then she **carries** up to 15 hatchlings in her mouth to safety.

crocodile

Alligators and **crocodiles** have been around for the past

55 million years!

crocodile fossil

An alligator can live around **30 to 50 years,** but crocodiles can live for **70 to 100 years.**

See ya later, **alligator!** After while, **crocodile!**

alligator

IS IT AN
ALLIGATOR
OR A CROCODILE?

1. An olive-colored reptile is spotted in the ocean. Is it a gator or a croc?

2. A V-shaped snout pops out of the water. Is it a gator or a croc?

3. A fast-swimming creature jumps high out of the river. Is it a gator or a croc?

4. Its jaw is closed, but its bright bottom teeth shimmer in the sun. Is it a gator or a croc?

5. A dark gray animal sprints along the shore. Is it a gator or a croc?

Answer Key: 1. croc 2. croc 3. gator 4. croc 5. gator